WHERE BROOKLYN AT?

gone – poems
 by ROGER BONAIR-AGARD

Willow Books, a division of AQUARIUS PRESS

Detroit, Michigan

Where Brooklyn At?

Copyright © 2016 by Roger Bonair-Agard

All rights reserved. No part of this publication may be reproduced, stored in a retrieval system, or transmitted in any form, or by any means, electronic, mechanical, recording, photocopying or otherwise without the prior written permission of the publisher.

Editor: Randall Horton
Cover art: Angela Davis Fegan

ISBN 978-0-9971996-8-0
LCCN 2016954831
Willow Books, a Division of Aquarius Press
www.WillowLit.net

Printed in the United States of America

For Nina Jane Merrill Bonair-Agard, forever

For a colonized people the most essential value, because the most concrete, is first and foremost the land: the land which will bring them bread and, above all, dignity.
—*Frantz Fanon*

I grew up on the opposite side / I'm not you!
—*Joell Ortiz*

Contents

1968	9
prologue	
Nina	11
Palimpsest	13
a foolish pleasure whatever…	
Where Brooklyn At?	23
Ghost I	24
Honorific	26
Where Brooklyn at?	28
Ghost II	29
The Bank	30
bossman	32
1110 Fulton Street / Bedford-Stuyvesant 1989	33
the black boy knows	35
How to be an Immigrant in East New York, Brooklyn	38
All America(n)	40
Ah say ah jes get de will from Lord Kitchener	
How it Probably Began	44
Fast—how I knew	45
pickup	47
Ghost III	48
The Gospel According to Trinity Street (Book 20)	49
The Gospel According to Trinity Street (Book 1)	50
Because I cannot remember my first kiss	51
Where Brooklyn At?	53
In defense of the code switch or why you talk like that or…	54
Where Brooklyn At?	53
Our Bodies are Made of Stars	58
Where Brooklyn At?	62
Dawn's Early Light	63
Brooklyn, one more Again	
Where Brooklyn At?	67
A pantoum for how not to gentrify	68
Bifurcate	69

claim—for the ocean	71
In which Jay-Z asks me to come back to Brooklyn	73
Niggas	75
Citation, or safe in Bed-Stuy	76
The Perfect Slice	78
City	80

     Epilogue

Coming Home	82
Things to take with you when you move 807 miles away from home	83
Where Brooklyn at?	86
coming back to Brooklyn (a Barclay's Center ekphrastic)	88
Acknowledgments	91

Foreword

Where Brooklyn At?! is something of a manifesto. It is certainly also—if a thing can be both—a protest song. It recognizes exodus and rails against the forces that move people before people want to move. William Faulkner's Anse Bundren out of the novel *As I Lay Dying* has a curious reasoning

> *When He aims for something to be always a-moving, He makes it long ways, like a road or a horse or a wagon, but when He aims for something to stay put He makes it up-and-down ways, like a tree or a man. And so He never aimed for folks to live on a road...*

To be sure, this collection of poems does not aim to reason by this logic, but it certainly believes in something like the right of a people to stay put if they choose. The global phenomenon of gentrification is kin to the phenomenon of Manifest Destiny, the triangular Slave Trade, white flight, the Israel-Palestine issue, and the ongoing, never-solved matter of American racism and classism. It purports to acknowledge—if not directly identify—a power, not of the people that forces the people's hands and makes exodus where exodus was not intended, and the collection intends to have everyone address the question in the only way these questions have ever been addressed in a way that offers the moved peoples dignity—through their stories.

In public popular intellectual discourse, the term gentrification is bandied about with regularity. To different folks it means different things. The supplanting populations often see themselves as being no less powerless than the supplanted ones, albeit often with more options born of the social cache of color or economic class. The supplanted populations know they have been fucked, even as they sell their own houses for cash, even as they see their neighborhoods visited with all the amenities they hoped for while they lived there; as soon as they're gone. To be sure there is not nearly enough discussion and analysis about how developers and real-estate puppeteers gerrymander all this pain for cash.

*As such, *Where Brooklyn At?!* is a collection of *gone* poems framed in the meta-analysis of the poet's own personal movings, beginning in Brooklyn gone to Trinidad gone to Canada gone back to Trinidad gone back to Brooklyn and now (finally?) gone to Chicago to see about his child—the sort of move that in some ways ends all restlessness. Or at least leaves one with the idea that he ought to be able to stay put; up-and-down ways, like a tree.

As with other poetic projects I've undertaken, the larger question—the philosophical, cultural, political one—comes first, and then finds itself incomplete without the personal excavation; the narrative that might round it out and humanize it. That the birth in Brooklyn of Trinidadian parents is part of the narrative—one of immigration, re-patriation and immigration again—is to complicate what the leavings mean and how they catalog. That one might be Brooklyn-born and come to know oneself as entirely Trinidadian is part of both a difficult story to tell and an unspeakable sweetness.

**As such, *Where Brooklyn At?!* is too, about how the various places have made me and thrust me away to find my way elsewhere. Always, the experiences in the one locale craft the man who must move on to the next, and change irrevocably for him, the place to which he might return.

***As such *Where Brooklyn At?!* is also poems of loss and leaving, the relevance of my own blackness and the blackness to which I belong and the nature of poverty and violence negotiated in order to stay alive and well through the leavings.

The collection almost towards the end of its first drafting, begins to feel itself address itself to my infant (and first) child, Nina. As such, it moves away from wanting to be a constant dirge. The collection wants to offer Nina something to claim in Brooklyn, even as Brooklyn becomes more and more the poster child of what gentrification and violent change means. The collection is aware that by the time of its publishing, even this understanding may have jumped the shark.

Faulkner's novel centralizes around a number of themes/events, among them, the transport of Addie Bundren's dead body back to the place she believes it should be put to rest. The role poverty plays in this journeying is of course the background against which all this tapestry is woven. Hopefully, it is not quite the tragedy of this idea that remains the lasting conversation from *Where Brooklyn At?!* but the more triumphant demand for an individual's and a people's dignity. Our stories are taken with us. Our stories also remain in the places we leave. We hope our bodies can be laid eventually in ground we can claim as ours.

Roger Bonair-Agard
Smoky Mountains, TN 2014

1968

I love my city, sweet and gritty
Inland to outskirts, nicknamed Bucktown
cuz we prone to outbursts
                    Yasiin Bey

burning
about to make a canvas of the city
burying Martin. Still burying
Malcolm too
my mother and father already beginning
to be history
            I get born
Spring
somewhere in the quiet dark
curled like a question mark
a figure screams his name in paint
on a train-yard wall

prologue

Nina

The bike shop used to be a bodega. The liquor store used to be a pizza parlor. This café used to be an Italian restaurant. That kiosk used to be Joe, an old man on a little stool. The yoga studio used to be a butcher's. The bar with jars of MandMs on the counter used to be a candy store. This park used to be a park—with crack vials and pot holes on the running track, and dirt in the center of the field where grass should be. And that dog run was a field of geraniums. The Dominican restaurant used to be cheap. Used to have a line out the door. I used to be able to afford to live above it and come down in the middle of the night and get half a chicken and a Heineken, especially after my girl left and I was tired staring at the linoleum and the sloping floors. The organic market used to be a sneaker store. Kim's grocery used to sell 40s. This subway stop used to be dangerous. Used to be able to buy crack here; right here. This coffee shop used to be a law office, run by Mr. Jenkins who chain smoked Newports whose family came from North Carolina in 1950. That sushi bar used to be the Jamaican spot. They sold patties, hard dough bread and the best sea moss. Those condos used to be a three-family house. I loved a woman who lived there. She cooked steaming pots of rice and fish broth and coo-coo and dumplings and stocked the fridge with Guinness when I came calling.

The bank used to be a quinciñera shop. The barber shop used to be your Papa's house and was once overrun by rats. We filled in the spaces between the steps leading down to what used to be the storage room, but was your Papa's floor. We clubbed the rats when we saw them. They screamed like children. The library used to be the library but no one from the projects round the corner goes there anymore. Saturdays used to be the Central American League where they wouldn't pass the ball to your Papa or your Uncle Cyril—the pool used to be empty. The Thai joint used to be the OTB and every morning, Joe, the old man on the stool walked there slowly, leaning on his cane, spent 50 cents for coffee in those blue and white coffee cups, and placed two 2dollar bets and went back to his stool and called out to me *Hey young fella* and told me how it used to be. Coffee used to be 50 cents, Nina.

Beat cops used to be in squad cars. They weren't always so polite. Biggie used to freestyle right over there on that corner, and Jay-Z came up right over here by Marcy, and Big Daddy Kane once played a block party here on Marcus Garvey, and your father used to be slim and ran these courts on Macon and Malcolm X. The New Casablanca bar and lounge used to be for old black people. Old Black people used to be able to afford this corner. This garden used to be a drum circle before the new neighbors called the cops to complain. Stuyvesant Heights used to be Bed Stuy—that family with the stroller used to be black. Those young people on the stoop over there used to be black and Puerto Rican and arrested for being on the stoop. That school used to be public. This used to be Brooklyn. They used to be scared to come here. They used to be sorry for us that we had to live here. It was a look like pity, like scorn. It looked like this corner and these bricks and this stoop. Brooklyn was what they left when they ran. Brooklyn used to be black, Nina. I swear to you. This used to be Brooklyn.

Palimpsest

I August 1987—Cascade

It was August, the heat swelling the pavement
into tiny bubbles. The day was here.
I was to going to New York—sent
to make the family proud, but I was a young boy nineteen
and all I could think of was the soft
hairs on the upper thighs of my woman left
behind, her mouth full as a breadfruit and more complex.
The night before, she wept onto both our tongues
and I promised, believing every word, that I'd love
her forever, that we would find our way together
again—America, Trinidad—some thing.
Curtis was gone. Randall moved back to Grenada
and nothing informed our grip, so much as grief.
In the six months before I was to leave, this woman
whose mezzo alto made the thickest hymns
in my ear, who smelled the way cocoa smells
in the bush, late in the morning when the air is lush
with rain and dangerous with the venom
of coral and mapepire, was all Trinidad was to me.
Her mouth was made of bubbling thunder
her skin an even charcoal and everything
she said, as certain as the sea.

But now, morning. My brother, almost ten
and I therefore still as infallible as the Sun.
Wailing loudly as we walk to the car
(my mother let us ride together in one car,
while she and my father rode in the other).
How I made it to the airport I'll never know,
through both our noise and heaving—
the tears blinding the road, the traffic
dizzying all the memories I knew
I was leaving behind forever, though no articulation
outside of my mammoth grief could have told me so.
I was in love still with my country—the rivers,
the mountains' precipiced roads, the rum, the heartbeat
of a Renegades engine-room, fat bottom black women,

small-goal football wherever we could catch it, Arouca,
Santa Cruz, Cascade, Sangre Grande, the smell of blood
in a forgotten gayelle, I was in love with the whole
thing and hadn't figured how to tell it before it cast
me off. A big big sadness grip me and it would take
me more than twenty years to sing.

II April 1968—Brooklyn

All of America is burning. My mother
and the woman who would become
my godmother share a long railroad apartment -
a single loft really, single beds
either side of the room. My father-to-be
is in Montreal, preparing to send a note back
to my mother saying I wasn't his – condemning
her to birthing me alone in the Angel Friends
Catholic Home for Girls. Brooklyn burning,
Detroit burning, Philadelphia, Chicago, Atlanta
burning and black and Martin freshly shot -
my mother alone, burning, birthing a black
boy in the bright spring. My mother's name
is a harbinger of spring, a harbinger of thaw.
Hyacinth's iced veins go home to tell her
Presbyterian mother she has made this
black boy and will bring him home, as soon
as she has a job. Her mother demands
she give me up for adoption and Hyacinth's
wail is a siren across the Caribbean Sea. She
is a banshee in memory of me, foster-homed
in Brooklyn, not yet one, not yet grown hard
as cedar wood in the Northern Range, not yet
learned to fill the hole in my heart
with gravel of my deepest ballading. My mother
and I both have lungs longer
than this entire archipelago of islands that wants
to hold us, that wants to sink our bodies like
it has buried so many black histories before.

III August 1973—Emperor Valley Zoo, Trinidad

A *boa constrictor* is lying asleep in a cage.
I can say this word because I can read well.
I've been told I can read well, so I read
everything out loud. *Boa constrictor*, says
the sign, so *Boa constrictor*, I repeat
over and over in time to its dark
belly, glistening and folded
in on itself. It is slick, gorgeous,
blue-green. I want to stroke its back,
its flank, its tucked head like a fat bullet.

A short gate is opened at the back of the cage.
A black black man wearing khaki coveralls
and rubber boots, shakes a bucket through
the short gate, and out tumbles a fat, white
rat. The rat runs to the corner of the cage
farthest from the Boa Constrictor and trembles
like the ring of bells on a belly dancer's waist.
I don't know what is going on, but something
seems wrong. I look up at Uncle Elvin. He says
It's feeding time.

The big snake scents something new and awakes,
unfurling, a canvas flag, slow
like incoming tide. I can hear
its big body drag a threat across the concrete
cage floor as its bullet head howitzers
in the direction of the small shaking beast.

IV. September 2012—Chicago

She says she's pregnant…

V. January 2013—Brooklyn

                  …after we know
                  it'll be a girl, Suheir
and I laugh at a coffee shop
on Franklin. *Look*, says Suheir
I don't believe that a woman traps
a man, but you ain't exactly freed
a nigga either. It's been some years
since we've been able to chill
like this. We watch
a very different Brooklyn walk
by the window, at the corner past
the C train & Shuttle stop at Franklin
and Fulton where crackheads swarmed
in the 90s, when that subway stop used to be
the most dangerous in the city and a white
face was nowhere to be seen, and no-one
called the cops to shut your house party
down, even when it went on until 6. *Yeah,*
I call that shit, the abstracted trap, Suheir
says, and we giggle our asses off
as a long-legged blonde woman
in Pro-Keds and a torn off-shoulder
Obama t-shirt orders a double espresso
over our shoulders. *This shit is wild*
we say, almost in unison.

VI. November 1977—Winnipeg—*the first time the white boys come*

Bless me Father so I may smite them in your name I may plague them in your name I may make blood flow and the bones break and teeth ground to dust in Your name Praise You from whom all blessings flow these fists are blessings these feet are blessings these elbows this tongue this fuck you respect me and my whole Black blessings too and make the temple of my mother's house a sanctuary for all things Black the exaltation of all songs their turntables prophesying break beats Black righteous defense and scripture I write in Your name in the name of self-defense and blackness Black in the temple my mother prepares for me at the cross at which my mother feeds me so that I may carry Black Forgive me Bless me Father and this dirt these lily faces that force me delay these swords from ploughshares become Your trumpet and Your wrath and know that this is love and God and Black and the beauty of the Son, the Holy Spirit, the God in Black risen up and chanting in service, and memory of You.

VII. August 1987—East New York, Brooklyn

The broken bottles in the parking lot at the corner
of Stanley and Van Siclen are hot to the touch,
but the breeze is a heckling
along the hairs at the back of your neck. You
lean up on the brick wall outside the corner
store like the other boys do in a white
undershirt, a tank top over khakis. You've
discovered only a week ago, beer
comes sometimes in 40-ounce containers which
cost 99 cents and so, that's what you drink.
Your Sony Walkman only plays *Paid in Full*,
headphones wrapped over your floppy
hat as you consider what moves you will
make. The money you saved and brought
here, is gonna be done in two weeks.
Tomorrow you're going to the Army
Recruitment center on Nevins.
You're going to answer that ad in the paper
for seasonal work in Alaska—any option
that suggests hard work for money.
You'll rack up some cash
quick, you think, and get started
on this college business. You drain the 40.
You head back inside
the bodega for another. Rakim opines
Thinking of a master plan…

VIII. April 1968—Memphis, TN / Bay Ridge, Brooklyn

A bullet leaves a rooftop or a bathroom
window. It doesn't matter
to the bullet. *I'm not worried* The bullet only
knows where its headed. It is
made itself of liver and marrow
bits of leaf, promises. The bullet
was once a prayer. *Mine eyes have seen* The bullet
wants the sum of the purpose
for which it is born.

A woman, alone, weeping, thirty
weeks thick with child, in a country not
of her birth, walks close to the stone
walls and iron girding of the Angel
Guardian Home. The oxidizing
turns the massive iron gates
a mocking green.

In the South, summer already -

the bullet leaves,
singing. The bullet
is made of wood and sweat
and wants to be ushered into
a small warm room.
to the mountain top… The bullet
is composing an anthem as it flies.
The bullet is going home.

The woman whose name is made of spring
looks up the marble steps, the brass
railing to the next set of massive
mahogany doors. Her sense
of smell, keen as an animal's, can
already detect the burning all around
her. At the top of the doors,
a single word—MERCY.

A foolish pleasure whatever / I had to find that buried treasure…
                                                  Notorious B.I.G.

Where Brooklyn at?

Take the 3 train to the second-to-last
stop. Van Siclen Avenue. Exit left out
the turnstile. Walk straight down the stairs
and into the witching hours of East
New York. Walk five steps and get your first
Walkman snatched from you right here.
The Sony doesn't bother you as much as the cassette
lost in the street tax – Eric B and Rakim's *Paid in Full*
You've been playing it on loop since
you got off the plane damn near, and
is your soundtrack to this new world
that is still deciding whether or not you belong.
1987 has turned on a dime and is about
to get directly in your face. Rakim say
Constant elevation cause expansion.
You've been robbed for the first time. Brooklyn
wants to see what you're actually made of.

Ghost I

The first time I loaded a gun it was Ed
who put the shiny weapon in my hand.
.44 semi-automatic he said. It was
heavier than an engine block.

Safety   Clip   Chamber Trigger

I was 19, a quick study
All around me, other boys
weighed instruments in their hands,
the whole room a choir
of steel-on-steel, crisp counter-measure
gear and grind, sliding into place.

*If anybody come here asking for me
shoot through the door*
                said Ed
supervising one more round
of my 3-minute tutorial of load,
chamber, safety. Earlier
he'd said, *Rog you can't go home
tonight. They finna war in these
streets. You gon get shot leaving
this building*. I was just too young
to wonder if I'd made a mistake
by calling on this kid's big sister.

But now all his soldiers present
all the guns inventoried - that
was the first time I'd seen a German
Luger or a sawed-off shotgun and Ed
dapped me up, and all those boys slid
like smoke into the night, and I lay
on the couch, barely sleeping through
the claps and retorts of fire in the streets
and on the rooftops. I awoke smartly
at every sound on the other side
of the door. Three-months deep
in Brownsville, Brooklyn, came courting

in the day, couldn't leave at night—ready
to make ghosts of anyone
who called
my new brother's name.

Honorific or *black boy to black boy*

Homes	Star	**Family**	Pardnah

Hollah   *what it do?*

My Nigga	Brethren	Ese	Fool

wha you sayin?

Black	Killah	Dude	Slim

What it look like?   *Wha happen now?*

Loco	Cousin	Captain	Playa

I see you…

Skipper	Nigga	Son	**God**

break yourself!   *what up?*

Blood	Gangsta	Horse	Man

stick em up

Homey	Boy	Dread	Nigga

As-salamu Alaikum   *you got beef?*

Taino	Money	Love	Young'n

Blessings   *where you stay at?*

Uncle	Joe	Friend	King

Who you rep?   *One Love*   *Freeze*

Rasta	King	Nephew	Lord

You 5-O?		*Alaikum As-salamu*	
Fam	Boss	G	Brother
	Oye		*Bless Up*
Nigga	**Nigga**	Nigga	Nigga
Aye		*Yo!*	
Nigga	Nigga	Nigga	**Nigga**

Where Brooklyn at?

Scared to death, scared to look
They shook
'cause ain't no such things as halfway crooks
                    —Mobb Deep—Shook Ones

at the Van der Veer housing projects
you call someone you know who lives inside
the compound to come out and get you.
No one visits Van der Veer without an escort
from the apartments. Young men carry
openly inside those courtyards.
We go to see Muff, perfecting the precarious
balance of walking without fear or challenge
through the gauntlet of black boys who whistle
back and forth across the quadrangle.
Under the canopy of that symphony
we brisk, without appearing to hurry.
We upnod our greetings without holding
eye contact too long. We wait at least
ten minutes after the most recent gunshots
before we leave to head back home.

Ghost II

The first time I saw a slain body
it was a boy from round-the-way.
He was 15 and I knew he was dead
before the detective showed me
the Polaroid of his bloated
shot-up face.

No-one said it out loud, but in our mannish
wisdom, we all *knew*
that the kid hadn't raped Tricia, Mikey's
girl. Everyone knew she fucked him, more
than once. But when the beat-down
looked imminent, she cried rape
and Mikey had to man-up, had
to not be a punk in front of crew
and family; customer and flint-hard
competitor. Mikey waited
in the stairwell of his building
where he knew the kid would
be returning early Sunday morning
from a night of selling Mikey's
product – and he clapped him up-
four shots to the head,
the fellas said.

We were all given our instructions
as to what we should say about Mikey's
whereabouts. In smaller cyphers
we regretted ourselves, said, *he didn't have
to wet him up though*. But what
choice did we have, standing together
in the cold, bobbing our heads to *Nobody
Beats the Biz* - the kid   already ghost;
1988, the War on Drugs in full
effect - all of us struggling
into mist

The Bank

like the morning I went into the bank headquarters and the lights were low and the old black military man sat me at that long, low table—and he smelled like Old Spice or Aqua Velva or something made of old men whose shirts were ironed crisp, and he asked you hard questions trying to make you lie on yourself—and the bulb hanging over the table was on a long cord like the interrogations on TV. I was 19 and the room was a warehouse—smelled of wet concrete—or maybe I imagined wet concrete because it was Manhattan and the building was nice and called corporate headquarters and it couldn't be wet concrete. Wet concrete was what you'd smell if you were never going to leave the room alive—if none of those doors led anywhere, or if those high ship windows at the top of the room let in those dusty shafts of light only for the reminder that you were alone in a foreign country, and had nowhere to turn, to run, and therefore had to listen to what the man said and make some things easier, and lie on yourself. Nah... that couldn't be wet cement. That was cologne. That was smug assurance. That was black retired military, in the pocket of whitey, playing a grim masquerade, an ill jumbie that I'd seen before—an evil I knew. There was only one way to defeat it. There was only one way to slay a jab-jab like that. You had to tell the truth, kill it with the truth.

> *I didn't take your money. And you know it. Fuck you for trying*
> *To make me say otherwise*

He had introduced himself as Mr. Roberts, Chief Investigator for Chemical Bank NYC Division, and for the first time the veneer cracked. Not like you could tell unless you were watching real close, but the jumbie froze for an instant, and inside my head even though it was cold outside I was playing a early morning midnight robber mas, my cape a-billow, hat broad and cocked forward and left and I knew the day was going to be my day, even though we hadn't yet gone to see the department head who said words like federal and jail time and we already know you did it because the lie detector test... but my outside words were low and constant:

> *Fuck you. Fuck you. How dare you? I don't need your money.*
> *I'm here to work and go to school and I don't care who the fuck*
> *You take me to meet next.*

The robber speech in my head was epic. *I am the first born of the black star on the blackest morning ever masquerade as night and I damblay on the beat before you know it to be beat. Step back when I burn because my cape glory like the first day the shepherds see the star, like the first day the snake offer the apple, like a basket with no holes carrying a baby in a river, like the Nile, like Africa before white people, like Mt. Pinatubo in full scandal, like the Ocean...* I was leaving my body the way my body had learned to ever since I was twelve. No, Mr. Roberts couldn't get me to tell a lie about myself to myself to these white men the way he had learned to, the way he had clearly learned to do every day so he got up in the morning to his wife's handiwork with an iron and put on a tie and saluted a flag and came to work to tell black boys to give their future away to his need to have a 100% case solution record. I was ready to meet his boss.

bossman

The office fluorescents fake daylight into the room as you think
of ways to slit the throat of the red-faced man across the desk

from you—a pen, a letter-opener, the angel-wing tips of a child's
trophy all line the mirrored mahogany surface between you. His mouth

is still moving, still accusing and already you've choreographed the snatch
and leap, the weapon in hand, the swift rake of the back of your fist across

his Adam's apple. You've choreographed the roar of his gurgling
surprised throat, the dark heart-blood rushing windy out of it and your own

high C of a wail—but the only thing that comes out of our mouth is *You cunt—*
I will kill your children. You are 19. You have been in America for three months.

20 years later, two books a literary series and learning your hands
to patience and tender in love-making, you won't exactly remember this,

when you kick the wing-mirror off the taxi and grab its driver by the throat
trying to yank him through his own window and onto the 5th Avenue

Saturday afternoon New York City streets. You won't remember exactly,
the disdain of the impossibly large, white man 20 yrs before, or his name,

James McHugh, at exactly that moment, but your hands remember. And now
you're not thinking of this man's children at all or why he won't go to Brooklyn,

or your younger brother's quivering voice as he begs you *Let go*
or your Persian girlfriend's *it's okay, its okay.* Rage

is like a river, now flooding the village of your scarred body, your broken
heart, coming back to shores hastily sandbagged to stem it. But rage

doesn't just keep babbling lazy to the sea—there's a screaming
man in a white van, one year—a bat in your hand, and his face

below it—a small man kneeling in a field, holding his kicked ribs another year,
a drunk man in a club—threatening you again, his face red—your body shirtless

and vibrating—the river swelling in this new rain coming down.

1110 Fulton Street / Bedford-Stuyvesant 1989 / a pre-gentrify ekphrastic

...jewels and all dat / the clothes was all dat
you think you steppin to me / that's where you take your fall at.
                    —Notorious B.I.G. (freestyle at 1110 Fulton)

See here—this corner bodega is where Biggie
dropped freestyle bombs before anyone knew
he was the Greatest Of All Time, before the police
started smiling at residents, before this bodega
started selling soy milk and organic toilet paper,
before it was a yoga studio before the blood
was scrubbed with lye and rock
salt off the sidewalk by the fallen boy's mother
before we paraded Biggie's coffin aloft through
the streets of *Bedford-Stuyvesant the livest one*
before beef with Pac, before white youth got
so goddamned brave enough to even ride the train
into Brooklyn, before slumlords fixed the toilets
and cleaned the lobbies and got rid of the rats
and didn't come to the building with thugs
to collect the rent, before Giuliani, even
before Manhattan got too expensive and chased
artists south who believed they were
the first artists ever to come here, because
that's always how white people Columbus
before the bodega let you come into the store
to buy 25 cent loosies in the middle of the night
and sold them to you through a bullet-proof turnstile
at eye-level from the street, before anyone
asked me for a credit check to rent a studio
they fixed the C/Shuttle stop at Franklin
and Fulton, before the end of crack or the Reagan
era, before Amadou Diallo and Dumbo
and Palladium was still there and Tyson champ
and NWA still together, and Left-Eye
still alive and they hadn't cleaned the vials
off the field we played on in Saturday leagues
even though families were there, and children
were being raised and the people demanded

good food and were ignored and were sent
patrol cars rolling their neighborhoods slow
and no one was so goddamned proud of themselves
because they planted a community garden and called
the cops on their neighbors with noise complaints
and boasted about the great West Indian food
and complained about how hard it was to find
tofu, *but the people here are so real,* they said,
and so alive, it was great to live here before
everybody decided to come.

the black boy knows

Bo knows this, Bo knows that
But Bo dunno jack
Cuz Bo can't rap
          Phife Dawg, A Tribe Called Quest

Yes I know, how to load
a 9mm, a .44 revolver, check
safety—off. I know

the djembe's goat skin,
   the tri-note of drum-kissed
  fingertips,

how to dance on the down
beat, and make pesto from scratch.
   I know how to play
chess, cricket, croquet
  and of course
basketball.

I know Mozart. Marley.
I know Biggie.

      I was once called the most
brilliant student in ten years
in my high school. I was the head
prefect.   I know
  how to weigh   heroin,
and I know a fairly detailed
 timeline of hip-hop history.

Yes

      I know women, how to make
     love, how to put
  my mouth to their centers
and pray.
I know hot
sauce from scratch. I make

rice and peas and I know
how to plant
        a backyard garden,
to dig a hole with only a machete.
And I know garlic
on the blade to make
the inflicted wound unhealable

I know how to throw a punch,
    how to build a kite
        from brown paper, bedsheets
        and flour & water glue paste.
I know how to tie a reef knot
  a timber hitch, make a splint,
recite the Boy Scout Law.

I know how to drag race,
        how to swing
a bat at a man's head
and not feel anything. I know
  how my own blood
tastes. How
my woman's blood
            tastes.

Yes
    I know
        how to walk
  on Melrose Place in Hollywood
on Southside Chicago, in Brooklyn
and how to slow it down in Arouca,
  or Kingston, or Castries.
I drink rum straight
without monkey-face.
        I have had to bathe
            a drunk friend.

I know
       how to rehab
my mother's tender
and new replacement

hip, how to talk
her down from the days she is still
 the girl given up for adoption, how to remind her
 of all the people who remember her name
I have not always known
that; or how to say
       I love you—
but I know how to hold a newborn
and how to care for the baby's
mother. Yes, I've broken a bottle
with all intention to confetti
         another man's flesh

I've hopped the turnstile.
I've punched a man and dipped
       through the back door.

I know what to say
   when I'm lying to a woman
   about another woman—Yes
I've driven 18 hours to tell the woman
I love I'll be hers alone
if she needs it. I've meant it
           and I know how to call Kevin
           and Patrick and Maureen
           when she says no.
I know how to want the hole
in my heart removed, how to speak

to a cop with his hand
on his gun—a stick-up kid
     with his hand on his gun
   my man Luis, with his hand
on his gun.
I know

my hand
my gun
my heart
      at half-mast   daring a motherfucker
         move.

How to be an Immigrant in East New York Brooklyn

Try not to let your old-country walk
bounce too high, your arms swing
too wide from your thin-hard body.

You come from a country of sweat and machetes

Men here speak in tongues
of gun-oil, the long music of drawn
steel.

You come from khaki and rum-talk.

Your mother did not teach you
to scent the blood in another man's
slick walk, his arms too close
to not be carrying at least two threats
of death with which you have not yet
been visited

Make your bed.

When a lanky man approaches you
in the shooting gallery sections
of Cozine and Van Siclen,

understand what it means to be loved
from far away.

When the lanky man is joined
by thick-torsoed men who almost surround you,

stutter-step stiff-arm and ghost
into the dark.

Full-tilt dip and juke away from the bullet
that never comes seeking you.

Be grateful for these men's love

though you will not know it
as love for another 25 years

Pray they never saw jail ,
had a liver, lung, spleen, begged
by another boy's inexpressible grief.

Reconcile your love for boys
who look like they could be
your sons.
Love even the fires dying to consume you.

All-America(n)

John, Temper's brother, little older than me, say
he don't wanna hear his wife say shit to him except—
and he mimics moans of sexual ecstasy and calls his own
name. We laid out laughing right next to the outhouse
all the tobacco leaf smell thick, thick in my nostril
from the field next door where we walked to go
see the Indian burial ground.

We in a dirt yard. In a corner, chitterlings
boiling in an old can. My woman, Temper
(real name—true story) thought it was time
to bring me down *South* to meet the extended fam.
We engaged—cubic zirconium ring—Crown Heights apartment.

And John finally turns to me and says *Rog
but… where you from tho?* And I explain,
Trinidad & Tobago, pair of islands all the way
south in the Caribbean, and John say *what part
of America is that?* So I continue explaining
sovereignty, using words like *independence*
and *island-nation*, and saying *six miles
off the coast of Venezuela*. But John
is confused, shakes his head impatient
like I ain't hear his question right, says
again *yeah, but what part of America
is that*, landing on the *that*, the *t-h* hard
as the *d* in the dirt yard—my own triangular
slave trade stop, to him, indistinguishable
from his own, so now I channel my people,
teachers all of them, think to myself *Brother
is a visual learner* so I break off the lowest
hanging dry branch from the tree whose roots
run under the outhouse and I get down in the dirt
to draw homie a map. I draw the fat spread shape
of America, its northern border like a shallow wok,
its craggy outpost of Atlantic shore. I show him the vague
mass that is Canada, and roughly point out the East
coast to him—New York, where we just came from,

DC, which we just drove through, *Virginia just North
of here*, I tell him, *the Carolinas where we are* I say.

Big Mama in the house making mashed
potatoes and fried chicken with the other women.
Earlier we'd left Manson (real name, true story)
town with no streetlights, town even the residents
of Durham five miles away can't locate; and hit
the Piggly Wiggly to get us each our own
personal flasks of Mad Dog 20/20.

John is half-nodding, looking on with a frown,
sipping his Mad Dog. I get to the hanging
peninsula of Florida, and I fancy myself Jesus
now like in the story of the adulteress brought to him
by the Pharisees, where he's drawing on the ground the whole
time. I'm like that, messianic in my lessons
        I show him Cuba, Jamaica, Puerto Rico—all countries
I'm sure he's heard of before, and I'm almost
in love with my cartographic genius now, filling
in the Bahamas, Martinique, St. Kitts, St. Lucia,
Barbados, Grenada and finally with a calligrapher's
flourish, I fill in Trinidad which I haven't seen since I left
the year before, and I'm thinking of beaches, and Marcia
to whom I made love at night at the edge of one of those
beaches on my birthday, three months before I left,
who as I was drawing was still mourning us, mourning
when I met John's sister at a bar
in New York City. I fill in the vague
silhouette of South America, next to the home I have
no idea when I'll see again, and I say *and here, John
here is Trinidad.*

Inside, Big Mama is telling stories about sharecropping,
her uncle who could dance his behind off, and *white
people back in the day.*

        The other men, bored have moved off, talking
about their trailer home extensions, car engines
crops, guns, women. It's almost quiet when I look
back up at John, who is slightly agitated now, squinting

at my artwork, right hand dangling at his side, thumb
and forefinger gently choking the flask's throat.
He points dismissively at the end of the drawing, says
yeah Rog—but what part of 'murrica is that—America
finally full of white people, and fields, and basketball
and highways in his mouth—America of chitterlings
and blues landing in John's beautiful song of a voice.

I look into the trees for something
I can't yet name. At the exact same time
we each bring a flask to our mouths. We
gulp hard.

*Ah Say ah jes get de will from Lord Kitchener /
You know de man did will me ah whole bag of soca*
                                        Scrunter

How it Probably Began

The book had pictures of real people
inside. Their bodies rose and fell
in places I had only wondered about
before now; only a mythical terrain
of what might be happening beneath
the canopies of blouse, jacket, skirt
coats. All the bodies pale in black
and white—and hairy. And something
in me sang out to the *breasts* and the labeled
vagina, and even the explanations of what
happened *when two people love each other.*
How could I love
learning and not love the body?

My voice rising, I asked for a brother;
wanted to know where they came from
that I couldn't just have one,
and my mother brought home the slender
bible *Where Babies Come From,*
thrust it without ceremony into my hands
said   *Read*   and all of a sudden
the streets opened, the bodies
of neighborhood girls became a gauntlet
of inquisition. So much magic
opening up to me that summer holiday.
I was skipping a class
Going directly to 2nd grade.
I noticed Monique's dark skin and sunlit
smile, discovered I could take a punch
and live.

Fast—how I knew

In 1980 I was fast. I knew I was fast because Muhammad Ali told me so. Said he was the Greatest of All Time. I still hear the phrase *all time* in Ali's voice, no matter who says it, with that exaggerated high vastness in his tone, his eyes crinkling up in the corner especially after Zaire, after Manila. Ali said *all time* and he looked like a benevolent king, ripe for a dethronment.

But it was 1980 and far as I was concerned that wasn't the time. He was about to fight Larry Holmes and win again. He was going to pull one more rabbit from one more hat and shut everybody else up again, even as other boys said he was too old and this latest challenger too young and strong. Ali had stayed too long they said, but I knew there was no such thing as too long for the G.O.A.T. Ali had run and chopped wood and prayed five times a day and was going to be great forever.

That day, in the pavilion, right after cricket practice, shirt off and dancing in my socks on the warped wooden locker room floor, I shuffled, showed the boys how Ali would do later that night. All 11 yrs, 90 lbs of me flitted around the room, clowning like Ali would. I was fast and pretty, showing off my tiny, quick fists and bobbing my head this way and that and talking, like Ali did. Too fast. Too pretty. Showing off my narrow unimpeachable body in the days before I'd inked a crown into my chest, a red butterfly where my heart should be. I was fast and Ali was and he was going to be heavyweight champion of the world forever, then all black boys could know they were fast, and talk slick to white men, and the world was going to open up. I was sure of it. I was a black boy.

My mother told me so. She'd let me stay up to see Muhammad Ali talk shit to George Foreman 6 years before, when I really thought he was going to lose and watched his body sag into the ropes, get pounded and pounded before he became some bullet-handed Jimmy Slyde, Honi Coles kinda super-hero and Africa chanted *Ali! Ali! Ali!* And it was late and I was leaned forward watching a thing I had never seen before, my mother getting up and dancing too, a slow hip-sway scotch-on-the-rocks- in-one-hand-not-daring-to-spill-shimmy and she sang *Oh God Ali, dey cyah touch yuh!*

So, see… I knew I was fast. I'd fought myself through the crucible of a Canadian Winter and learned how to pretty up my rage and dress it in something shiny and cocked to one side and my thin, tiny body that healed so miraculously and would wound and scar back to brown again so easy and walked anywhere it felt like past any group of boys, knew Ali had enough left to beguile this bullet-headed man, Larry Holmes. Everything was going to be gravy, *Ali Boomaye!* all over again, even though my mom was tense now and my father working. Late. Again. I'd just finished practice and learned a new stroke and made some runs, and took some catches and everything would be right. Ali—king of the world, greatest of all time—he was still young and fast and black. And so were we.

pickup

This is how we chose teams—2 boys
not necessarily the best ones, but good,
boys we all liked—each one selected
from the gathered throng, the best, then
next best available, until the last boys
were left and the selectors threw up
their hands and said *okay well I guess
I'll take you too*. And even that last
selected boy broke into a quick trot
to join his teammates for the game
that day, accustomed as he was to being
picked last, but sure that he would get
to play, be passed the ball, allowed
to shoot, have a turn at bat. We all knew
where we were being picked more or less
depending on the game and weren't
each of us then just as sure in raising
his hand and calling for the ball
gimme, nobody on me! even with
a defender draped on our backs?

We were so cocksure of our successes,
failures, our teammates saving-grace
tackles, or brilliant catches.
What a short glory in our lives,
when we knew we lived
or died as one extended body
that we'd fight and be fought for with equal
snarl & leap. We bloodied
our knees, fists and noses in praise
of this, and raised glasses, and walked
to our homes—tired, alive, unafraid.

Ghost III

for Cyril

Lunchtime in the back of the classroom, in the empty
space on the old half-rotted floorboards back of what used
to be the library; boy & ball, ball & boy, we pushed
back & forth outside of foot, in, outside of foot, in;
our sneakers making tiny whipping sounds, like quick
dry brooms. Sweat punctuated the ritual, first left foot
then right, left then right. Maybe we had seen Ian Clauzell
do this first, or our own Sandy, or seen Gip perfect it
late one evening before we decided to take the beating we knew
we'd get for staying in the courtyards to play, past dusk.
Or maybe we'd sat, like me, with an uncle many years before,
to see the Brazilian, Rivelino, who laid claim
to its invention, while my uncle, Keston, a legendary
philanderer, who later I'd see bend a free-kick around a wall
past a keeper who stood frozen, drank a tall beer with ice in the glass.
Keston insisted I watch with him even though just six years old,
this man with the thick mustache and curly hair—
Rivelino & Keston - put the elastico, the spanner
on hapless tacklers. 1974, and the Brazilians, defending
champions, without Pele, Jairzinho or Garrincha for the first time
in twelve years, and we, eight years later, back of the class-
room, black & hollering at perfection for the first time,
cussed when it didn't work, but went right back at it.
Nothing to do with our lessons was ever practiced this
Diligently, no chore ever performed with such attention
to detail. We stopped in moments to tie our shoelaces,
to laugh at another boy's attempts, to draw our breaths
in sharply when one of us got the ball to move so swift,
it seemed a ghost—here one second, the next
                                    smoke. Once
our bodies were, like that—haintlike in our quickness
and building a magic, a ritual. Now you see us, now -
shadow we had only just begun to name.

The Gospel According to Trinity Street (Book 20)

He has said his morning prayers; had a simple meal—tea from the yard to fight the little cough he feel coming. He pick it early, dew still on the leaves, dark still unmoving from the dirt. The wife has risen with him, though they sleep in different rooms now, and though she not so brisk in the kitchen any more she still fry up the sausage nice nice and her bread when hot is still a little bit of Jesus when the butter steam on it. All the khakis, all the shirt jacs hanging in the closet already pressed. She does all that on a Saturday so he just pull a shirt out, white crisp, starched over the merinho, tucks the khaki pants into some tall boots and goes to see about the cocoa. It is still a dull, steel gray in the sky when he leaves with a flat and a brushing cutlass inside a crocus bag wrap up and heads towards Tamana. He thinks it is nearly time for the boy, his grandson, to learn about this land. But for now let him sleep. Let him study his book. He still young. He must yet be taught and churched by the women. The taxi man is the same one he get most days he head to Tamana so they exchange one or two pleasantries, Morning, how you do? Look like it set up to rain. How the children? How the garden? But the old man has never been talkative so is mostly silence till Grande where he will change for a next taxi to go up in the bush. This morning the cocoa ripe. Some men already harvesting so he make himself busy instead with clearing the brush underneath. He begins immediately but takes his time. You must be brisk but you never have to rush when you clearing your own land. The long handled cutlass swipes clumps of grass from right near his feet, whistles a perfect arc back into the air and comes round again in a full circle to swipe the next clump held in place with the crook-stick in the left hand. This certainty repeats for more times than he can possibly count, and as it does, he hums songs soft in his head, mostly hymns, chuckles from time to time to remember something the boy say. He is bright and strong that boy even though he thinks they let his hair grow too wild. Without looking at his watch he knows it is twelve o'clock and time to stop; has cleared brush from the road all the way back to the river where the land descends into a soft reddish mud. Here it is cool. The shady immortelle even more plentiful here. He unwraps a pristine kerchief, soaks it in a brook, and presses it against the back of his neck and wipes down his face. It is here he knows the land best. It is the only moment of which he tells no one, not even Father in confession. He has something to leave for the grandchildren. It is his 81st birthday and he will work the land till he can walk it no more. This is the only place he has ever allowed himself to cry.

The Gospel according to Trinity Street (Book 1)

Some Sundays the roar of the motocross rose out of Garden Village like a prayer chant. Get close enough and you could see the bikes leap with a high-pitched scream out of the muddy valleys of the track. They leapt like dolphins. They leapt like rumor did in that way they congregated there round the track, the way those rumors ringed the basketball court in the rectory yard, or the pavilion at the hot flatness of Undaunted Grounds. Always testing our speed or daring we headed in groups of four or five to the games there—always me, Anthony and maybe John Khan. There were other groups of four or five always about, a whole village moving in a wave like religion towards the center, towards whatever event held us in thrall. And the village —Ms. Lukus Babb drunk and cussing at 7 am every morning, the exodus of Grassanto's goats (or were they his ghosts?) from Boundary Street to Main Street and beyond the flat slap of Grassanto's feet on the hot blacktop, loud and drunk in the mid-afternoon, mad Cyril Henry's midday antics, brain recalling the body's scholarship as he paced from his house to Arouca Boys R.C. School each day. Arouca was intelligent and whimsical. It was a legend of a village, yielding both champion scholarship and remarkable depravity. And all manner of story made home there, from the Golden Grove prison to the Lopinot Hills, from Five Rivers to Garden Village, whether soucouyant sighting or Henry's brilliance (before he turned crazy) to Father Rodriguez' famed exorcisms (he would ride off on a motorcycle). And the parties at the Lodge was as good a place to pick up a woman as church on Saturday nights, and Boland's rum shop was as good a place for an argument as graveside on All Saints' evening, and when Arouca became ground zero for Trinidad's crack epidemic, we whispered that the village was cursed, the inhabitants becoming zombies before us even as our best friends raised their children there, but that the children we'd seen grow up stole from our houses and boys we'd played cricket with in the street turned tricks and became beholden to a monster which in turn moved like a tenth plague through and amongst us, and Arouca must indeed be cursed by the Carib cacique who had to give it to some conscienceless conquistador, so we were doomed always to hear chains rattle at night, have our most brilliant lose their minds or leave altogether, the earth itself curdle with cruelty. But look again, the spread of real estate, golf courses to the village's south and north, the murders multiply the gunfire louder than any village carnival. The air is electric. There are spirits rising everywhere.

Because I cannot remember my first kiss

but I remember sitting alone on the brown
couch in my grandmother's living room,
the cushion covers made of velvet
and the color of dark rust, or dried blood
and sewn by the tailor from up the block,
the same one who made me my first light blue
suit two years earlier.

I sat there running my hands back
and forth over the short smooth hairs
of the fabric and understanding what touch meant
for the first time—not touch, the word,
as in *don't touch the hot stove* or *don't
touch your grandfather's hats* but touch
like Tom Jones was singing it right then
on the television, with a magic that began
in his hips, swiveled the word and pushed
it out through his throat into some concert
hall somewhere as a two-syllabled sprite,
so that women moaned syllables back in return.

And I knew I wanted to touch
like that—because
Tom Jones stooped down at the edge
of the stage and a woman from the audience
in a leopard-print jumpsuit unfurled
from her front row seat, walked like
a promise (of what I couldn't quite
discern) up to him and pushed her mouth
soft and fast up against his mouth
and they both cooed into his microphone
mouths still move-moaning together
like that for an eternity.

And then Tom Jones unlocks
his mouth from hers while my breath
is still caught in my throat, and moves
to the other end of the stage, and squats there,
and kisses another woman from the audience

in a black jumpsuit, while the first
woman looks on, swaying so slightly
I almost can't tell (to the band
which is still vamping the chorus line),
mesmerized and taut with expectation as I
am, palms down on the velvet-haired
cushions. And Tom pauses, sensing
the first woman's impatient almost-mewling
and says *Easy Tiger* while he moves his mouth
against this woman's, his cheeks working
like tiny bellows, before returning to the first
one. And then the bridge or the chorus
or whatever—at that point the song
is an afterthought - and I knew there was
a mission to be fulfilled. Tom Jones
pointed to the women and said *touch*
and the new color TV made everything
shimmer with promise. My eight year old
body preened and stretched itself ecstatic
against the couch and dreamed
of what tomorrow could be like if I could make touch
mean so many things, if I could make
a building or a body coo like this.

Where Brooklyn at?

On Sunday mornings, Shirley
who works at Planned Parenthood
tells her fiancé she is headed off to church
and comes over to my crib. We play cds and we
make love in Bedford-Stuyvesant. She brings me
a carton of condoms because she says
let's none of us pretend you don't need these.
Shirley is so beautiful I don't know
why she is here, with me, but I take
care with her body. I also lose myself
in her the best way I know how
in 1992. Years later, when I'm ordained
through the internet, I'll decide I ought
to know something about the bible.
I keep returning to the story of the adulteress
being brought to Jesus on the beach.
So much of the story is for me. No part
is for Shirley, the realest part of Brooklyn,
several kinds of church.

In defense of the code-switch or why you talk like that or why you gotta always be cussing

I'm pretty certain my people Yoruba.
We speak drum and dust.
We are barefoot. We are also Mumbai
and the venomed thin blood streaks
of slave masters in France, England,
Spain, Portugal, Germany, America.

But my mother taught me *The Hardy Boys*,
the word *precise* and *Where Babies Come From*
She say read Walter Rodney. She say read Kamau Braithwaite
She say read Baldwin.

Long Before Chicago taught me borders
and *Joe*, what loose squares are,
the hieroglyph fist twirl dance
and gang sign,

my high school principal, Winston Douglas
said *It is a sin against God
your parents, and yourself, so to profane
the gift with which you were born.*

And so I learned the English
of John Milton, Derek Walcott
and the Mighty Sparrow.

But Brooklyn say *Sun* and *Godbody*
and the streets of Arouca taught
me the brilliant run-on elegance
of the eloquent cuss—*Fock You*
with an O so deep and round
you could tumble into the greeting.

Ruby say *not poncho; rebozo*
and bit my bottom lip
and cried when the moon was full

Melana say *ghost-pose* and Nita
say *it raining horchata*.
I talk middle-finger, nigger,
son, and espouse
on the theoretical and practical difficulties
of blackness as lived experience,
a meta-physical longing akin
to madness—and Northside say

*You're so articulate. Oh my God.
See—Look, even white women love you*
and the books say I code-switch,
say I double-tongued, say I adapt/
able. And I say I don't switch
shit. Stop trying to crack
the code and we'll stop (maybe)
inventing new syntaxes for
survive; for making paper,
for stacking cheddar, for getting
our money right. Switch/nothing.
I say I contain several
kinds of niggas—because I know Hindi
words for eggplant, rolling pin, machete,
and several kinds of cloth folded to drape
the oiled body of a woman. I say *Love*

when I talk to a woman, and I say *Love*
when I greet my homies, and *Family*
to address a sweet sister in the street
and *black* when I mean all my people
and *dead presidents* because Rakim,
Biggie, Jay-Z, Nas and The Wu Tang Clan
added vocabularies to the throng
of me. Chicago jails school me

BD, traphouse, swag, pole and bundle;
school me, you could be 10 years old
thrown to the ground arrested
in school, so I talk like *precisely*,
greet my gods with the deep O
of a well, of a drum. I speak barefoot

and folklorico, speak J'ouvert morning
and Toni Morrison. I recite Winston
Douglas' *never sacrifice principle
for expediency*. I holler at my boys
with a complicated-ass handshake.
I say *Horse*. I say *Blood*. My brothers
answer back. I sing. I lift every
tongue. I speak drum fool. I speak
drum, homie. I speak drum, dawg. I speak
drum, god. I speak drum, nigga. I speak
drum, *Joe*.

Where Brooklyn at?

In the summer of 95 me and Cyril buy cheap bikes
and once every other week ride from Flatbush
to Coney Island to hit in the batting cages. We ride
the go-karts even if we're the only two there.
We often go on a weekday afternoon, so we can drive
the ball till our bodies can't stand the shock
up our arms anymore. In the summer
of 95, we play football in three different
leagues. We take the train to the city
on the hottest day of the year. We drink
beer and watch women walk by. We
never wear shirts. We troll Prospect
Park for pickup games wearing our
most raggedy gear, so we can dominate
unexpectedly. Whole weekends get lost
and won this way. We can't imagine
any other life.

Our bodies are made of stars

A molecular cloud, sometimes called a stellar nursery if star formation is occurring within, is a type of interstellar cloud whose density and size permits the formation of molecules. —Wikipedia

I'm going back to Brooklyn, the stacks
and stacks of houses stacked on houses
the police cameras mounted on tree houses
mid-hood, the youths' heads all davening
to one massive downbeat, deconstructing
in their bodies every molecule of sound
so that they make of those bodies
a re-imagined God when they burst
anew with re-strung energy.

I'm going back to Laventille, the shacks
stacked precarious on a North Trinidad hillside,
where you can hear at every moment
culture being born and born again in steel,
in the rumble deep inside an old oil
drum, a new chrome—making sound
of re-designed anger. You hear the boom
of automatic gunfire, the slide of chamber
the unmistakable smell of sooted steel
too. That is sometimes how we
burst, kept tight under the pressure of some
inter stellar force swirling around us
and then we are…

Astronomers today believe that a large
fraction of the atoms inside our bodies
were once stars, that became supernovae
that were then launched into the universe
when these stars exploded. They're half
right. But they don't know how we turn
right back around and make the universe
when we explode—when we emerge
from cloud and doubt, new and fiery
with outrage, with languages
these larger bodies cannot decipher

In La Horqueta Trinidad, a housing project
(we call them schemes in Trinidad)
moved people from enclaves
with names like
John-John and Never Dirty, starts
at the main highway and moves section
by section (called phases) deep towards
bush, in places named Talparo
and Brazil, the sort of villages
named by people the city councils couldn't bother
to grace with running water
or electricity. In Phase 6 down
where we were afraid to venture
even in 1987 when we were young
and unafraid, we once saw a man
with no teeth, blunted higher than
an interstellar medium, do things
with a ball, barefoot, in a La Horqueta league
football game, games which often
ended in gunfight; which moved
us to proclaim him the greatest
footballer we had ever
seen. This league which national
players sought when they wanted to be
anointed as real, as stars among stars
forming and burning out right here
in Phase 6 La Horqueta, a man barefoot,
gave no thought to the cleats of his opponents
and scored at will…

The poet has been saying
for years, warning really
that we've got niggas with wings
and stars for limbs in the most unlikely
places. We're making the world.
Wouldn't you like to be in it
and made of star matter, of new
and shooting brilliant gas, made of us?!

The poet has a poem to write.

He is obsessed with what words
put under pressure might yield.
He is lucky in this pursuit of meta-
meaning. He is in a business
which allows him metaphor.
The research says he must holler
at something called a *young
stellar object*. Some days, the blackness
writes itself . Naturally
a *young stellar object* hangs
out in a *stellar nursery*
in its earliest stages of evolution.
Stay with me: the YSOs,
cuz we stay signifying like this,
are divided into *massive intermediate
masses* and *brown
dwarfs*. Sometimes
the blackness…

I'm going back to Brooklyn
to Biggie Smalls, a bridge for sale,
to Michael Jordan's birthplace,
to No Sleep till…
to the afternoon a 12-year-old dunked
on me in a playground in Bedford-Stuyvesant
back when white people asked me
if I was scared to live there
and I answered *No, I'm scared
of you*, you who drag black bodies
to rivers, who hang neighborhood
interlopers, who fifteen years later
moves in to the center of the starburst
I made my goddamned self and calls
it Stuyvesant Heights. Fuck you!
I'm the stellar one, been under
pressure and making explosion after
explosion out of the clouds and into
the universe. I'm the star-builder.
La Horqueta, Laventille or Brooklyn,
this is where the pressure lives, where
our bodies learn to streak blue-hot,

where we move from stardust to
trigger-finger to supernova again.
Wouldn't you like to learn how
to be a part of how you get to be
whole? To meet God?
To be born again?

Where Brooklyn at?

as a resident deep in sentiment they shout
Go Brooklyn, they representin it
Sittin on they front stoop sippin Guinesses
Usin native dialect in they sentences
                              Yasiin Bey

On Church Ave and 39th Street
on a Friday night, Burrokeets DJ plays
the most recent soca. Flatbush massive
gather deep in the small room and the session
is a sweet sweatbox. We get down low
Footsteps stamping harder, Footsteps
Feet together, Footsteps, spread apart
whenever a drive-by shooter sprays
the make-shift club. In unison we come
back up when the bullets stop flying.
Almost no one goes home. Trini massive
keeps drinking and dancing. Everyone here
is in mourning for a home left, is consecrating
a home claimed. We drink more. We grind
in the dark. We take lovers home.
We return the following week.

Dawn's Early Light

Bustin caps in the mix/ rather be judged by twelve than carried by six
                                              Ice Cube—Steady Mobbin

I'm flat down on my belly on the floor—summer now. I'm 24 in New York City—Brooklyn, first apartment of my own, second floor corner dwelling, amazing light, North West corner of Malcolm X and Hancock. Windows all the way to the ceiling on both outside facing bedroom walls. Hardwood floors—$250 a month. It's 1992 and I don't know who Jay-Z is yet, but tonight Ice Cube is loud on the cd player behind me. *4, 5 niggas in the mothership, better known as the goose and they all wanna smell the shit...* and I have to turn it down to investigate the boom I'm hearing outside. It's July 5th so kids are likely finishing off the M-80s and bottle rockets they still have left, but the sound is too insistent too steady; like all the DJs in all the dancehalls let the beat drop off the break at the same time. It's Bedford-Stuyvesant so I Navy Seal crawl my way to the window, and lift the bottom right corner edge of the curtain slowly. My lights are off so no-one in the hood can see me looking. Again, Boom. Middle of the block. Two men, one of whom has a shotgun he's firing off towards the South East Corner of my same intersection from halfway down Hancock West of me. Bits of brick chip and crackle off the building. Flashes of fire, maybe asphalt kicking up close to the boy taking cover at that wall, now slid behind it, now sliding out of cover Uzi in hand to spray the block in the direction the men are shooting from. For two minutes it goes on. Maybe it's an hour. There's no time now, only bass, snare, bass, snare, bass, snare—*fools get drunk and wanna compete / slap boxing in the street*—Cyril is upstairs in his Dad's crib. Frank isn't at the barbershop and there isn't yet a wine bar here or doggy day care where the scaffolding is in the middle of the block down Malcolm X boulevard between Hancock and Halsey on the east side, where the 48 bus lets out, directly opposite where I get my hair faded once a week and a part down the middle, like Larry Johnson, when he still had hops.

More automatic fire; and youngblood makes like he's gonna run south on Malcolm X and I can't tell you what I'm feeling except that I'm still on my stomach at the window, breathing slow. It's late. I was thinking about whether to go to bed or go out again when the street music got popping. I've had a few Heineken down at the New Casablanca Bar and Lounge on Malcolm X and Macon and rubbed up on a loud woman from Marcy Houses whose three kids were home sleeping, and she'd pushed her ample backside into me as we slow grinded along to Super Cat's Cabbin Stabbin, and she felt my erection on her so she'd reached back in the dark to squeeze my dick but I didn't bring her the four blocks back to my crib. Didn't even tell her I was leaving. Just got faded and staggered out, and now was maybe wishing that I had. But homie up the block drops the shotgun and comes toward the corner where in ten years my girl will come up in the middle of the night to see me, her hair dyed purple to match the half slip she's wearing as a skirt over her combat boots. Cops will exasperate her by always asking if she's okay or knows where she is and she'll answer *do you know where you are?* But they'll still offer her a lift out, which she'll decline.

But brother approaching the corner, giving it a wide berth as he does so, has what from here looks like it could be a .38 semi automatic and I startle myself by recognizing it from this far. He turns to go down Malcolm X after the youth, except he can't see that homie is hiding behind the scaffolding half a block down. And this is where maybe I could shout or whistle something out the window, but that ain't the code for this part of the world. It certainly isn't smart, so I stay quiet and get to see him get five feet away from the kid's spot before the kid steps out and calmly offloads 4 or 5 shots in his stomach. And he falls face first; timbers—dead before he hits the sidewalk, his face turned slightly to the right as it smashes into the concrete with a crunch right there by the bus stop. And right on time here comes the 48, second shift off work and the man's blood hasn't begun to leak out from below his body yet, so maybe they don't know he's dead. Maybe he's just some drunk on the sidewalk because they all step over the body and go on their way. First, a nurse in her gleaming whites, next a construction worker, hard hat still on and then some teenagers who keep looking back at the body like they're not sure but they head up the block and turn right onto Jefferson. And the bus pulls out, the driver not giving the body on the sidewalk a thought, and in less than a minute the street is quiet again. The dude who buys his crack from the spot up on Quincy and then smokes in the empty lot on Hancock, across the corner from Malcolm X, runs to the body to see if he can help and as he does, a red hatchback Sentra screeches round the corner the vanquishing boy leaning out the window, his body from the waist up, shirtless, outside the car, back leaned against the edge of the car's roof—and I'm thinking about how thin he is; from here I can see the young man's ribs - and he keeps his finger on the trigger for about five seconds and the crackhead screams and slides, luge-style under a car parked on the side of the road. By now *Giving up the Nappy Dugout* is almost done and I can hear the high hat whispering down the corridor back of me. And the car is gone out of sight down Malcolm X. I can hear the exhaust almost all the way until Fulton I think.

I still can't move from my perch by the window, and for the next five minutes the streets are crazy. Men and women are running out of buildings and houses, and everyone has a gun. Lots of 9mm, a pearl handled .45, a sawed-off shotty, and everyone seems confused from up here, shouting instructions, looking this way and that, asking outloud about about where the shooter stay at, and even more wildly it's about ten minutes before the police show up. I almost can't hear Cube, *Do I gotta go sell me a whole lotta crack for decent shelter and clothes on my back?* and it's the sirens come in. I'm not sure for a second if it's a sample from the CD player or the world outside my window, but everybody fades against the dark unhurried like when a slow jam comes on and there's no girl left for you to lean on. Just as easily though, folks fade up into the lights as the police inspect the body and the ambulance is there a split second later, and a woman with a blue headkerchief alternately screaming and cussing *where were y'all? Where the fuck were y'all?!* at the police who 20 years later will give me a ticket for peeing on a fence at 4 in the morning two blocks from here, and 10 cops will show up to watch me, while a young white couple walks past arm in arm giggling drunkenly and looking amusedly at the scene. The woman is inconsolable, so the man with the pearl handled gun which I can still see peeking out the back of his waistband from here, has to bear-hug her and whisper something in her ear so that the grief-throttle coming from her throat is all low church and gravel now, and he sways with her while she moans into his chest, and I want to block out the semi-circle of residents around the body and the police and the EMT, and imagine that they're two lovers, in the corner of the New Casablanca grooving to Al Green, as he turns her away just before the cops nod at the EMT and he draws the white sheet up over the corpse's face.

Brooklyn, one more again.

Where Brooklyn At?

Nena has a gold Glock pendant, guns
tattooed on her forearms, a voice
like gravel made of stones worn smooth
by the sea. She pours drinks deep
in the long narrow bar on Grand
where I go three, maybe four nights
a week, and many mornings. Nena
will let me nurse a single vodka and write
for three hours. Mostly, she'll top me up
with Ketel One and tell me stories.
Around us row homes get sold
and life long businesses get bought
out. Nena says *fuuuuck* under her breath
a lot at new faces in the neighborhood.
But she's crisp behind the bar. Nena
calls me *sweetie*. I'm in love with women
who tend bars anyway. We go out one time.

A pantoum for how to not-gentrify

Huddled around an engine, hood up, in winter
hoods up, low-voiced and dropping verse
and chapter about pistons and crank-shafts,
young brother inside takes the signal, hits the gas.

Hoods up, low-voiced, dropping verse
on the corner of Fulton and Classon, hand claps.
Young brother inside takes the signal, hits the gas.
The cipher gets deeper, bass croaks from a throat

on the corner of Fulton and Classon. Hands clap.
Taxi screeches to a halt, soca out the window, like a flag
deep in a Flatbush cipher—bass croaks from a throat.
U-turn, and the lyric inside is smooth negotiate—peace.

Soca out the window like a flag when we stroll Nostrand's
black soap, sugar cane, shea butter, ites gold & green.
And the lyric outside is peace—a sooth negotiate
to all the slick-handed, dapped-up sidewalk economies—

black soap, sugar cane, shea butter. This natty roots hat
is how we shop for household items in black Brooklyn
from all the slick-handed, dapped-up, sidewalk hustlers.
Mornin tantie, brethren wha happen now. Love, cousin

is how we greet our fam in black Brooklyn.
Interlope here, and look my people in the eye, learn
Morning tantie, Love, cousin, wha happen now brethren -
love languages that could free you, from your skin.

Interlope here and learn, before you impose, fam.
We built the beat you came here seeking, craft
love languages that could free you from your skin
if you join in—if you make yourself the not-center one time.

We built the heat you came here seeking—
pistons, crank-shaft, manifold, its entire engine—
join in and one time make yourself the not-center.
Huddle around, hoods up, nod your head. It's winter.

Bifurcate

Western Main Road, noon. 90 degrees,
St. James hopping. Brian picks
me up from the TV station,
and we run the streets. At *The College
Bar & Grill*, legendary snackette,
I hop out from the bass-throbbed
car to buy four cold *STAG*. We will drink
the first round fast enough,
to require the second immediately.
This is one way I honor home.
I salute Trinidad like we all do -
with waters.

Two old fellas at the bar—dark,
leathered skin, flip flops & tank tops,
look me up and down. We know,
always with a glance—who come
from foreign. They speak loud
about me from three feet away

—Dat is de young fella was jus on TV6.
—Eh heh?
—Yessss man, we jes see him talking bout den poetry an ting. Yes now, right dey
—Oh ho!
—Look at he face good. I know him from right here in St. James

and this is how home claims you.

But I'm thinking about Brooklyn
about the summer—about how I don't
make it back to carnival anymore
because Black History Month—in Brooklyn
I'm Black—landlords spit in the dirt
where my footprints have been.
In Brooklyn I'm Black and angry
and home and not home.

—Yessss ah recognize de boy face—ah know him good
—Used to lime on Long Circular Road, on Bournes Road...

this is how old men reclaim
their own youth—even on the other side
of the country from where you grew;
from when you were barefoot;
your country is a gathering of ideas—
doubling up on drinks, bathing in bass
on the way over the Northern Range
to the beach—I'm on my way
to the beach—my woman recently left
our apartment—so now the linoleum
floors and fourth floor apartment
and hipsters moving West are mine too.

I'm losing two homes at once.
I'm being claimed twice.

I one-love the old fellas—they're on to
cricket and football now—I grew up here
at the corner sometimes by *Smokey & Bunty*.
I climb back into the soca music.
We're going to pick up sun-salt-kissed
women wrapped in sarongs
head to the beach—eat fried
shark—I have two more days.
I belong to Brooklyn. Brooklyn has began
to spit me out. I'm going to kiss a woman
I belong to Trinidad. Trinidad claims
my birthright all askew. I'm going back.
I can't go back, I'm a man
building a country
of his own. I have no army.
I leave the only flag I know. I return
to Brooklyn—the Republic—I'm Black.

claim—for the ocean

for John Vietnam
for Patrick Rosal

Vietnam drowned in a lake last year. Pat say
that's why he don't fuck with no fresh
water. Pat say only ocean buoys island bodies
enough for the risk of the moon in the early
morning. Pat say nobody brown need
to be fucking with a lake—at night, no
less. We toasted then—*tagay tagay*
Filipino style—to Vietnam, to his body
claimed away by a vexed moon's tide
even though Pat didn't even know youngblood.

*But what about all the brown bodies at the bottom
of the salt water* I say. *Damn son, no doubt*
Pat says *tagay tagay*—we toast again. Ocean
claim so much, we sit up in Brooklyn
drinking a rum from Hispaniola, from
sugar cane, talking bout we only fuck with salt
water, like we done give Ocean all permission
to take as it see fit. We black/brown; ironic
as fuck, half ready to fight the next white
face we see—half weeping into a full glass
of rum before we empty it and pass it
back to the other.

In this ritual, you don't pour
your own drink. It is respect to fill
your homie's glass, and be poured for
in turn. It is a celebration ritual, a grief
ritual. One night is about a boy I loved
claimed by a lake—another, about finding
the foster home where I was born, before
my mother had to cross an ocean to prepare
a place for me, before I crossed it and crossed
it back again to find myself black and besieged.

So many of us bones blanched at the bottom
of this ocean, and still we take to it like
it loves us, like we family these 500 years
of float later.

Ocean don't love us / It just love our mermaid style,

but I don't tell Pat this part. We're drunk
by now and inside our own heads, floating,
deciding what to surrender
to, and what to leave submerged.

Once, on the island that made
me, the ocean was a ritual
too. I climbed mountains
in an old car in the middle of the night to make
love at its shores, to remember where I had
come from so that it might stay
with me where I was going. That night
the water came up, lapped at our bodies, furious
in the sand. We wept.

We filled
each other's cups. We put the ocean
to our mouths.

We drank.

In which Jay-Z asks me to come back to Brooklyn

In the dream, me and Jay-Z slapbox
like boys do—actually we say it's okay
to throw punches because we believe
we can't really be hurt. We strip down
to undershorts. We take our shoes off. I believe
I can beat him, but he's a big dude so I'm a little scared.
I don't want to get caught by a big random punch.
You gotta take off those rings I tell him.
He laughs, takes them off. One of them is a graduation
ring from my high school. *You have a QRC ring?!*
*Yeah pahdnah. I heard about your work. I got one
When I filmed that video in Trinidad in 2000.*
That's fresh I say. We start dancing
around the room. Jay's wife shakes her head.
It's not Beyonce. It's a local girl he stayed with.
They have two kids. We'd been hanging out
earlier. She took me to meet Jay. She leaves
the room. We flail at each other. No real blows
land. Neither of us is going in hard. I'm thinking
I need to get inside them long arms so I can hit
him with a flurry. I know I can end it quick
if I get inside one time—crack him in the jaw.
You should take that ring he says. *Your fingers
is way bigger than mine. Paus*e, I say. We laugh.
Jay's wife is sitting a ways off under a tree, knitting,
talking to a neighbor. It's Brooklyn but not
Brooklyn. In another part of the dream
I have a frustrating conversation with an ex
and then I'm mad I haven't stuck to my plan
to never talk to her again. I'm back with
Jay-Z. By now, we abandon the slapbox.
We're breathing heavily and sweating.
It's time for me to go. *We gotta get up*
I say. *No doubt*, he says. *Come back
to Brooklyn fam. We need you.*
I wish, I answer. *I've got a kid.
Gotta get back to her.*
Bring her too, he says. *Brooklyn
take care of y'all. Here's my number.*

Gimme a call. We dap up. I hug
Jay-Z's wife. They stand close to each
other and wave as I leave. Everyone
is a little sad.

Niggas

(for avery, tai, miste)

We spin the yarn, use the word like nexus,
like we build a next us out of mis-appropos
out of rooftops from a Crown Heights they still
tryna take from us. *Niggas*. We use it
fluent as memorized prayer before
the smell of grits & fried fish gets too good
and interrupts the Lord under our intentions.
We see color, nigga, and so we know every
story under the leather and cable knit
of Billy Dee Williams' smooth-haired swag.
Dat's a nigga for real and we know it the same
way we got taught early that it don't matter
how tall or how rich or how gotdamned
learned we get that that word is ours
by back-break and lash and the love
we've had time to build and measure
in that room. That word migrates with us
to say slow, to roll around our mouths
like a tough sweet black toolum till
even our mouths are black with a nigga's
sweet meaning, with all the ways niggas
make to say Church, with how we sure
nuff gonna find our own way to glory

Citation, or safe in Bed-Stuy

Maybe it was the absurd sight of a helmeted man
pissing on a fence. Maybe, that it was a fence
separating the sidewalk from a playground. Maybe
it was because it was 4am and everything wrong
happens at 4 in the morning—every dumb story
every fight that ended the night at the club
when I was young and these streets not yet
worth policing. But the bright eyed fresh cop
boy sliding up to say *Hey buddy* must not recognize
I'm twice his age, or that I have my dick
in my hand. Maybe he and his partner haven't yet
processed the sleek, white-wheeled, bullhorn-handled
bicycle leaned up next to me, before he asks
the next dumb-ass question—*Didn't you see us there?*
And for two seconds my drunk brain is aflight with
all the unsmart things I want to say—
Yeah I saw you, I wanted to show you my dick.

Nah, I didn't, but I sure am glad you're here now.

*Yeah I actually was trying to piss on your shoes but I'm too drunk
to aim right,*

but only the self-preservation me speaks

But the pig won't relent. He's got a treasure trove
of questions like these he saves for 4am,
for grown black men on Quincy Street,
Bedford-Stuyvesant-on-the-come-up-
hood-type-joint while he hoofs
his beat. *You couldn't hold it, huh?*
And I'm worried that there might
be a little smile on my face now—19
year old wise-ass me showing up late
with cocaine and tequila to fuck the party up.

And he and his partner are so not yet
old enough to legally get the kind of drunk
I am right now, but they're one thumb

nonchalant in a belt, one-hand-casual—
on-a-service-revolver type sure of themselves—
and the one barks something into his radio
and is oinking something about how he could
give me a much worse citation but he'll let me get off
easy, *but you shouldn't pee in public* blah blah blah
like I ain't been potty trained several years before
his parents even thought to fuck each other.

And the couple that passes by just then, not even
noticing the commotion, shouldn't need to enter
the poem except just ten years ago, the police
wouldn't be walking the beat here—just cruising
by in squad cars and asking my purple-haired,
combat-booted girlfriend if she was sure she was
in the right place. But tonight that cop is just
as sure the tittering blondes passing just behind him
are safe because he's got this under control.

And then, almost silently, a murmuring among them
like a group of Jesuits on the way to mass, ten more
police show up, their shoes not making a sound,
and they stand around while babyface runs my ID,
and I'm thinking that isn't it something, this is really
how it's gonna go down, beaten to death by cops
in Bed-Stuy or maybe my life saved by my bicycle
helmet like everyone always says it would, and my
little girl in her mother's belly still, will never meet
me. So I try to hold the gaze of the one black cop,
a woman, young. I hope she sees her brother
standing here, or her man, or her father. But she
looks everywhere except my face, and her thumb
is tucked in her belt too, and her hand, resting
on the 9mm like an afterthought, all of them doing
their jobs, polite and casual—in Bed-Stuy, finally
to protect, to serve.

The perfect slice

I'm six gins in when the Midwest transplant
boy in the thick-framed glasses
tries to argue with me
about the best slice of pizza
in Brooklyn. I don't live here
anymore, and gin is a recent
habit—as a lover assured me—an old
man's drink. And I don't know if
I have what it takes to thump the 20something
and the two years of capoeira he picked up
in the Peace Corps,
don't-know-his-place interloper
from Wisconsin trying to school me
on the perfect slice.

But this is how a city starts to leave
you - brick by brick. Or rather, this
is how the Republic of Brooklyn claims
itself back from me. I turn
the wrong direction at corners now—another
awning, a stoop, fading from memory.
Whole months in these dark streets called back
to the borough from the sweet honeycombs
of my remembrance. In this Brooklyn
of the perfect slice, my woman and I
brought blood to each other's skin—
it rose there like tide against my brow

I let another love full-swing
slap my face and rattle
my teeth to atone for what is obvious
now I had no right offering—
I ducked through parking lots
and the cavernous underbelly of project
complexes to avoid the chain-snatch & beatdown
the police and *Decepticons*; and this boy's
cavalier culinary critique does not belong
in my Brooklyn where I asked a beautiful woman
once to be kissed under a full moon

and she laughed, touched
my cheek, refused my mouth.
I remember her locs against my ear
—my own pleading, weeping—
the rum we'd been drinking inside
the house, the almost sheer white
floor-length dress rivering over the black
valleys of skin, the weed boys heckling
from a corner away—
all under siege
by Wisconsin's opinion

and the boy is still droning on
not just about the perfect slice
but how to tell if the slice is good,
the crust, thin; like he ever had
to lay a napkin on top the slice
to soak up the extra oil, to know
if that way he was really on to
something that would keep the liquor
in his belly, at bay.

So I just stare at him
like I'll hit him anyway, and offer
nigga, fuck is you talking about?!
as a way to court Brooklyn back
to me—here for a weekend drink
at a bar that wouldn't be here
ten years ago—and wouldn't you know it?
Wisconsin boy shuts up, having no sensible
retort to being called *nigga*
by someone obviously willing to be one
just then. And wouldn't you know it?
Brooklyn comes back to me,
calls me *Baby,* buys me a round.
Bar is quiet now though, and Brooklyn
makes it clear, it is not falling in love
with me, ever. It knows how I do.
It shows me the moon.
It refuses my mouth.

City

    House of love, house of knives and dust and women with smoke between their thighs. City do what city say it do—city money & blood. City so *Brooklyn*—city stay shirt off waiting for summer front yard cold beverage and a girl I love. City family and city don't give a fuck. When I say city rumble, I mean the J train. I mean the 38 bus. I mean the click-clack of a spray paint can. City people on top of people on top of people in a building on top of a bridge under which more people. City frisk niggas. City try to stay white but city can't stop the shining. City praise Jesus. Scared of everybody else. City so night and city so sparkling. City skin smooth as Africa, smooth as *its* cities, smooth as hunger and mango peels. City walk swaggerific and talk slow- city signify and three-card monte. Several times city try to break my arm my spirit, try to bullet my lung. I too fast for city. City too slick for me. City asks no quarter, gives none. But city dance; and when city dance, city heal. City music. I mean this is what city do. City. Stay. Music—and so city love me more than I can love it back. Sometimes I city and then I am both fist and my father's laugh, both taxi cab and skid mark. Skid row. Skin pulled back and black-top beat down. I said city white right?
    City bright. City bright. City bright. City shout louder than the night.

Epilogue

Coming Home

Brooklyn comes back to me now
with all the wonder of a phantom
limb, reattached. The corner's rhythms
making their way back into the body
stanza by stanza. Look there's the bodega,
the Laundromat, the liquor store, the sneaker
store, the liquor store, the bodega, the bodega
the Dominican breakfast spot, the St. James
Church of God, incorporated, the liquor store,
the bodega—oh, a new French bistro. Seems
I can close my eyes and find all of these
by walking a requisite number of steps
in any given direction. Even the lope
of my fellow Brooklynites, the one that
re-enters me in these blueprint swaggers,
is familiar again—its own hat-tilt and head-
nod, its own wave across the block, its own
disaffected gentrifying too-cool hipsters.
And look: *Russell loves Tinamaria,*
OddFellow, OJ "Left" in bubble letters
—the graffiti waves back. The writers get up
everywhere, and in desperation. It's how I know
I'm home again. Everyone is in a little bit
of pain, and making it look beautiful
as a sunset in a smog-filled sky—bodega,
liquor store, liquor store, bodega, the High
Times Church of the Christ Our Lord and
again, the darkest hand-styled scrawl,
Tina, I miss you. Come home.

Things to take with you when you move 807 miles away from home

A drum, a Masaai spear, 2 frying
pans, a three time bought
copy of *My American Kundiman*, clothes pins,
an acoustic guitar, red Pumas
with the white stripe, black
Pumas with the black stripe, silver
Pumas with the yellow stripe

the pictures of me—still looking out my back window,
I'm going to meet my daughter or my maker, depending
on how you call God, god.

the green coffee cup Vicki gave me,
the ceramic pipe Alex gave me,
the dominoes Thuli gave me and the imagining of teaching them to my
daughter, the tiles just small enough for her hands when she first learns to
slap them on a folding table and pray out loud,

Selected Poems by Derek Walcott,
Omeros by Derek Walcott,
White Egrets by Derek Walcott,
the black bicycle with the red
stripes and green handles leaned in the lobby,
knives,
a Yankees cap,
a White Sox cap,
Brooklyn on three caps,
a green fedora with a feather worn
high on the head, like a rude
boy, like the knives are sharp

Jack Gilbert's entire oeuvre now spread out on the bed next to a lover. I
need all this, and the slow weeping of dinner, and the succulent pork and
eggs and chicken and noodles and herbs from my friend's mother's yard.
They made me feel strong today.

The Lucille Clifton poem that ends
*Everyday, something has tried to kill me
and has failed.*

Take the last stale cigar, the half finished tin
of Bustelo, the photographs of the lover
with the ornate tattoo at the base of her spine
or rather, the photograph of her feet
One Hundred Years of Solitude
with the cover torn off
the promises to the ex-lover to read
the entire thing to her.

Take the black bear coat from Milica.
Take the broken watch. Take
the carving of two lovers entwined. Take
the black sleek sweater, the sheepskin coat. Take
Bushwick and the slap of your flip flops on the sidewalk
to the Laundromat back with you. Take
the upnod, thug greet to the brothers mid-block.

The poem has always been a field. Since Frost, these prosodic, precise
lines meant to grow things out of their fallow, always our uncles, fathers in
that field marshaling one death or another. Take the yoga mat, the white
candle you burned on New Year, the first draft in pencil that stayed on your
nightstand and made you remember whom you hurt most. Take the brand
new bottle of lubricant, the new sleek black shoes with the red laces, take
the kettle bell and the barbell and the smell of that last lover on your sheets

What is the news that interrupts?
What is the death that intervenes?
What is the nature of joy and surprise if not to have
the plough diverted from its neat and reverent lines?

Take the car seat, the diapers, the rocker (for the girl),
take the Dr. Seuss, the blue onesie, the diaper bag (for the girl),
take your father's excuses (for the girl),
take the copy of *Head Off, and Split* by Nikki Finney (for the girl),
take Audre Lorde (for the girl),
take the last Sunday morning in Brooklyn, with Mahalia Jackson
on repeat. Take Nina Simone singing *Ne me quitte pas*, on repeat.
Take the lover and you curled up and reading everything you could find

I want to walk them the new shoes into a field where my father is ploughing and tell him how I once dragged a boy down the stairs, how I tried to drag a man out of a moving car, how I threw my arms open like I was receiving an ovation, as I leaned backward out of a speeding car and tried to make mush of another man's face. I want him to know his absence ordered their deaths. I do not know if this is true. My blackness co-conspires in everything. Take Amiri Baraka's *Somebody Blew up America*. I am my father's fourth child of six we know of. I am the news that interrupts, the ghost who carries his shoulders into war. Take the bicycle with the white tires, the fast one, (so you can get to the girl). I am walking into the field to tell my father that I love him, no matter how many carcasses he bids me fetch in the dream.

three love letters,
a small caliber gun,
a thick-mouthed lover's kiss as you leave for what feels like forever, as you leave your heart, leave Brooklyn, leave the graffiti that said come home and the memory of the nights you stepped over the dead before police made it safe for others to come into your hood,

a five-dollar crucifix,
a fresco of St. Christopher, the patron saint of travelers,
or maybe that's St. Jude in there, the patron
saint of lost causes,
the curled copy of her sonogram,
a picture of your own hands,
a picture of your father,
a blanket bought in Germany.

Where am I going? What is the nature of the field? What am I moving towards if my plough stays straight if I keep looking over my shoulder for the girl to come, so beautiful
in her brand new
shoes. Her shoulders are
powerful. She has done
as ordered. Her hands
(the ones you're moving toward)
are brimmed in blood.

Where Brooklyn at?

Dumbo to Coney Island
Red Hook to Cypress Hills
Brooklyn at Saturday afternoon in summer
police execution on the corner of Church and Nostrand.
Brooklyn at Labor Day parade *wine dong*
on Ocean Avenue back when we had less
police than masqueraders and no one
got shot. Brooklyn at Russian league football
at Red Hook. Brooklyn at the boardwalk
because… the Ocean—and this is where the sun
is largest, where there is still room
to pray. Brooklyn at Barbey and Broadway
9mm to dome. Watch took, $11 gone, you're cool
as the midnight itself, until you get home
collapse, cry inside the door. Brooklyn
at *The Cellar* on a Friday night DeKalb Av
crowd heads dipping in unified downbeat
until the adhan of A Tribe Called Quest
gets everyone facing the booth and hollerin
I left my wallet in El Segundo. The tallest
sister there stares you down for the next
groove. You spend the night with your forehead
against her ear her wide mouth thick at your neck.
Brooklyn at running outside in December sleet
to the corner phone booth cuz your homegirl
paged you, and said let's go to this poetry
reading and you're good with being lost
so you say *fuck that I'm watching ESPN*
but she screams at your ear. So you go.
Brooklyn at the abandoned Greenpoint
loft where you sit in old church pews
and hear the gospel of a kind of verse
you recognize. Brooklyn at where your life
begins to be saved again. Brooklyn at Biggie's
coffin aloft in the streets. Brooklyn at Junior's
cheesecake. Brooklyn at beef patty & coco bread
on every block. Brooklyn at the call to prayer
on Friday evening leaving out the mosque
at Fulton and Bedford and floating toward

Fort Greene. Brooklyn at Williamsburg—Bedford
and North 7th, 1989—ghost town. Brooklyn at
why that shit is funny now. Brooklyn at Los Primos
yucca, mangu y queso frito for breakfast 3 times
a week. Brooklyn at the best Dominican spot
in the city is right under my apartment. Brooklyn
at the landlords say the apartment is gone
when they see my black face. Brooklyn
at the landlords who let me stay
for seven years with no rent increase
in East Williamsburg. Brooklyn
at the windows I smash. Brooklyn
at the gun I stash in my waist twice
before going out into the hot Bushwick night.
Brooklyn at the full moon on my dome.
Brooklyn at the prayer I offer for every black
boy I walk by until I get home.

coming back to Brooklyn
a Barclay's Center ekphrastic

Because I love poetry, the specific poetry of black
bodies in flight, or mid-turn appearing to snatch god
out of the air or turn it into pure speed—because
I've always known these bodies didn't come by
such Grace through magic, through some trick
of light against our bodies' gleam, but work
and the obsession that turns work into glory
into milk and honey, into the effortless walk
on air. Because I've seen that obsession turn
into adulation and scorn and also nothing more
than unspeakable beauty where no more than the gathered
few will get to witness—and because I've found the discipline
in spots for such obsession and trained my body
to do things which then—thank all the gods—I got
the opportunity to do one or two times in my life
in front of small crowds who briefly chanted
my name or pat my back or offered me a drink.
And because of the many places I'm from
I proudly number Brooklyn among them
and count as my Brooklyn bonafides the basketball
courts I ran from East New York to Bedford-Stuyvesant
to Flatbush to Crown Heights late 80s to early 90s
when I could still briefly grab the rim on a good day
or outsprint my man on the outlet anywhere
or hit my man a pinpoint chest pass the length
of the blacktop—I didn't beef when I heard
there was a stadium coming to moor itself
right in the middle of downtown Brooklyn.

And even though I knew that this is when
you know the neighborhood is finally turned
and men who love money more than they love
stories were now in charge, those stories
are what keep me alive, the stories of all people
always exodused from their homes and sent to seek
a place to call their own where they might plant
a tree and stay there long enough to have their grandchildren
eat its fruit. It is the most fundamental story

that keeps me walking and laughing and constantly
in love and kissing my child on the face more
times a day than she can stand; that black bodies
obsess on their ability to catch the light at exactly
the shade of gold it needs and hold it against
a hip for eternity, because most days it is the only
control a black body can still count on. Oh bless
oh curse the guns, the shell casings marked with the shadows
of our sons and the stories they tell when we die
and are reminded that our murderers are innocent.

And because the story of black obsession with body
gave me Muhammad Ali and Edwin Moses and Pele
and Eusebio and LeBron, I wanted that stadium
and the bodies in it gliding up to the rafters
and walking on air. I wanted their stories—
each individual tale of the come-up
from this hood or that or whatever suburb
saved a black life because his body obsessed
enough to make whiteness covet the idea
of owning us again—and because Jay-Z
American-dreamed his way from the Marcy projects
up to that moment—a beautiful American
robber-baron of a story, I turned the corner
at 5am re-entering Brooklyn, having been gone
for three years, to see the stadium's big ship
lit up body anchored so right between Atlantic
and Pacific, that my breath made a sound
at my throat like when the storyteller gets to the part
about how the slaves got free because they
sang the songs and obsessed about their Africa
and not their chains but their bodies, and climbed
high enough to leap off a cliff and eventually
fly. And though I know who really owns that
stadium and that team, I knew the concerned
citizens there protesting the stadium's coming
had erased the stories of people who'd
been there before—erased their stories in the same way
their white flight parents wrote themselves out
of it two generations before. And because the
Post then called Jay-Z a *n***a. And the cheerleaders*

might as well be b*****s, it said, I wanted my
body a part of that body, to belong to it, it
belong to me, like I claim hip-hop and Biggie
and Flatbush and Bed Stuy and East New York
and Williamsburg and Bushwick and the A train
at Hoyt-Schermerhorn and the 25 bus on Fulton
and graffiti only visible from the J train and any bridge
emptying into the county of Kings—this story, still
ours—still our bodies stilling the air and making
the light strobe through us—still so
gully, so ours to own, so Brooklyn

Acknowledgments

Poems in this collection have appeared previously in *Pluck!: Journal of Affrilachian Literature*, *Crab Orchard Review*, *Provincetown Arts*, *Drunken Boat*, *Academy of American Poets—Poem A Day*, and the anthology *Break Beat Poets: New American poets in the age of Hip-Hop*.

Thank you to *Willow Books/Aquarius Press* and Randall Horton. Patricia Smith, you continue to make me better. Thanks for the edits. Patrick Rosal, my brother—ditto and a thousand thank yous. Lynne Procope thanks for continuing to support and love me. Paul Seres, ditto. Maureen Benson for always helping me reach new parts of my head; to Joseph Basilo.

Queen's Royal College Massive in Chicago and NYC: George, Tom, Brenton, Arnim, Cyril, Gary, Ricky, Lenny, Stanice. Rich Ramkeesoon too. And the rest of QRC Massive back home. Mr. Douglas, I am doing as directed.

Chi-town family that stays holding me down. Kevin for the early look at the poems, Krista, Avery, Kristiana, Quraysh, Toni, Cheryl, Angela, Bill, Andy, Cara, Tyehimba, for some of the fiercest holding me down. Free Write Arts & Literacy Massive, always more than colleague and cohort: Ryan, Elgin, Mathilda, y'all already know. Let's keep building. Thank you *Urban Gateways*.

Thank you to Alice Oleson for always reading and pushing us both. Lauren Alleyne, for supporting and loving and staying ride or die.

Thank You eternally to *The Writer's Hotel* and *The Watering Hole*.

Brooklyn clan: Shade, Olufemi, Simi, Uncle Femi, Wally, Ayambi, Celia. *LouderARTS* family that still holding me: Guy, Rich, Eliel, Tish, Erin, Syreeta, Eric, Mahogany, Jive. Maaaan, y'all don't eem know. Greg Pardlo—salutes Sir! Suheir, you already know. Cheryl Boyce-Taylor, for space in our hearts and space to live in the liminal space, love. Willie Perdomo—bloch-uh! Lauren Ash, Thuli Zuma, Alex Ustach—I can't say enough. Colin Channer, Staceyann Chin, Kwame Dawes, I keep coming back to 1999. Thank You.

To my *National Sawdust* family holding me down and in particular, my *Vision Into Art* family and always collaborator and indispensable human being, Paola Prestini. To my *Miyamoto is Black Enough* brethren: Jeffrey Zeigler, Andy Akiho, Sean Dixon. Let's keep making this better. Milica thank you for your always support of this work.

To the world's best baby mama, Lydia Merrill, Thank You.

Arouca massive! Cleo Julien, Andy Perez, and the original soldier, Anthony Perez, and Michelle and Josiah! Always love. Larry Olton, still love!

To my partner and brain sharpener, Mathilda de Dios. More thanks and more building to come.

To my father Roosevelt Williams and the line I'm just beginning to know. I am grateful, and enormously glad you're here.

To my brother, Jamil. We still making ting, meh boy!

My mother, my mother, my mother, Hyacinth Lucille Bonair-Agard. Nothing I can ever say here will be enough.

To the boys and girls still detained at *Cook County Juvenile Temporary Detention Center*, and court involved and to all youth still fighting for their lives, and resisting a police state. #BlackLivesMatter.

About the Poet

Roger Bonair-Agard is a native of Trinidad & Tobago and Brooklyn. He is the author of three previous collections of poems, *tarnish & masquerade* and *GULLY* (both from Cypher Books) and *Bury My Clothes* (Haymarket Books, 2013) which won the Society of Midland Authors award for poetry and was long listed for the National Book Award. He fronts the band Miyamoto is Black Enough, and is co-founder of NYC's LouderARTS Project and Chicago's The Baldwin Protocols Series. The Director of Creative Writing with Free Write Arts & Literacy, he lives in Chicago and is Nina's father.

www.ingramcontent.com/pod-product-compliance
Lightning Source LLC
Chambersburg PA
CBHW021134300426
44113CB00006B/427